EXTREME DOT PUZZLES WITH OVER 15000 DOTS

DOT TO DOT PUZZLE
BY **MODERN PUZZLES PRESS**

DINOSAURS

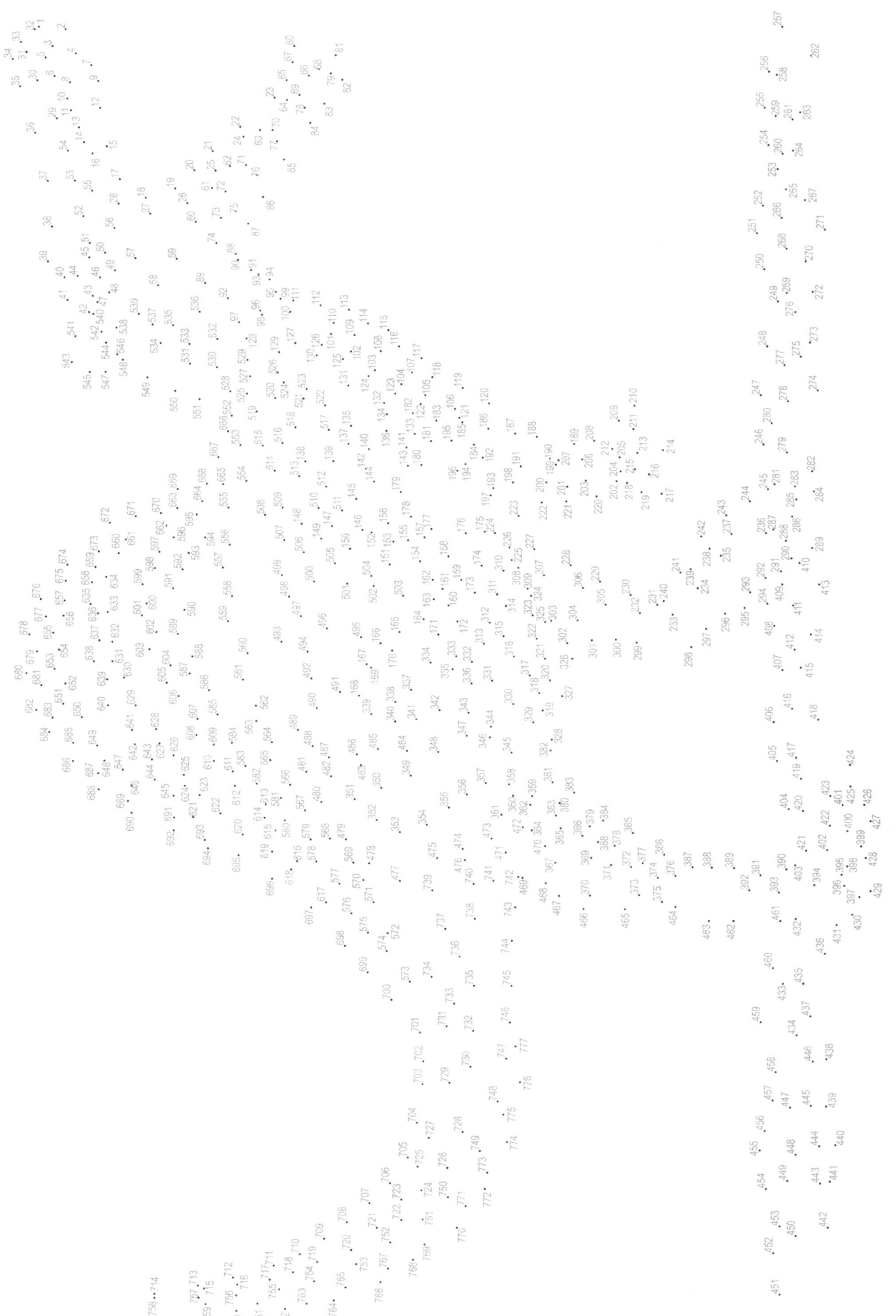

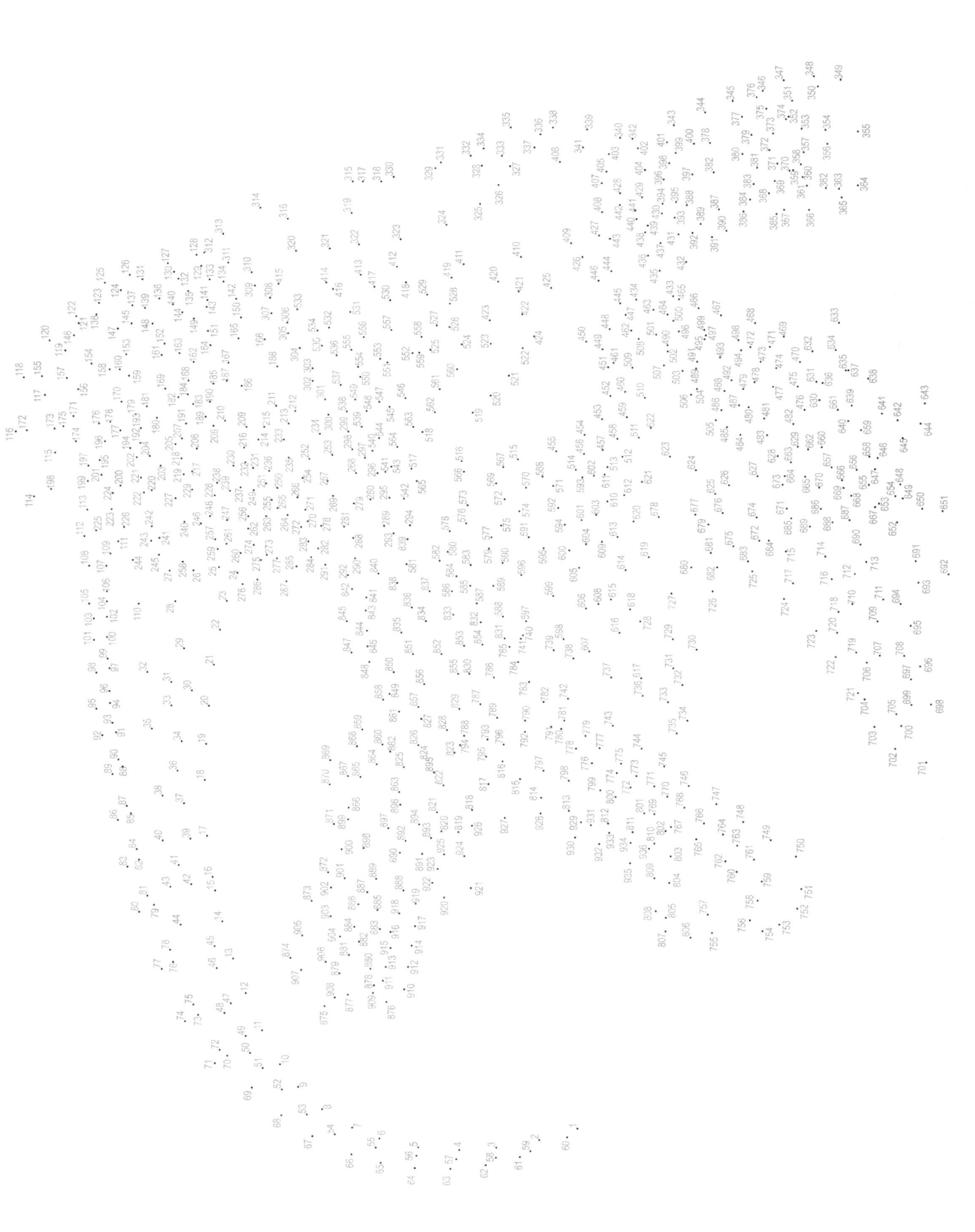

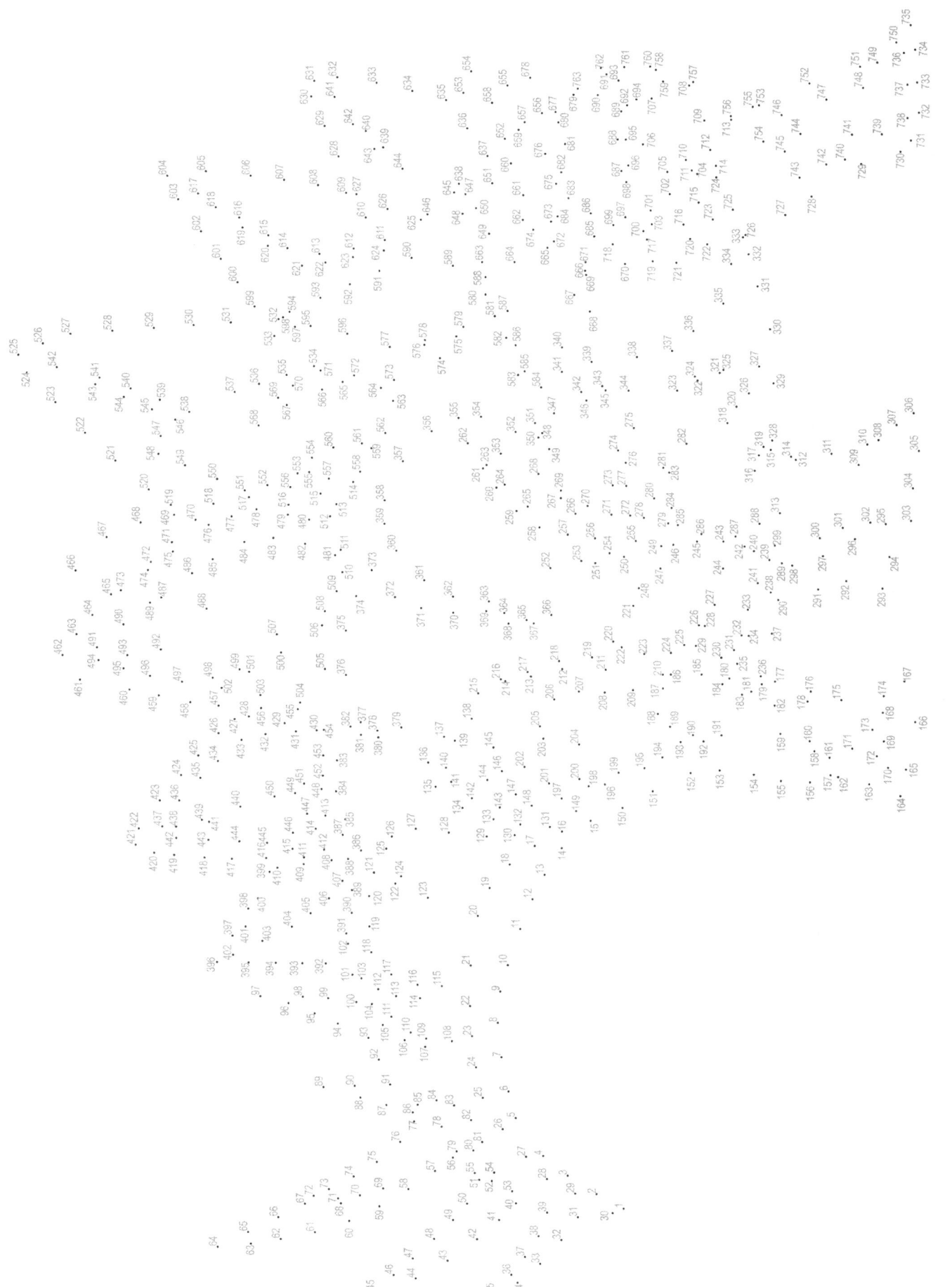

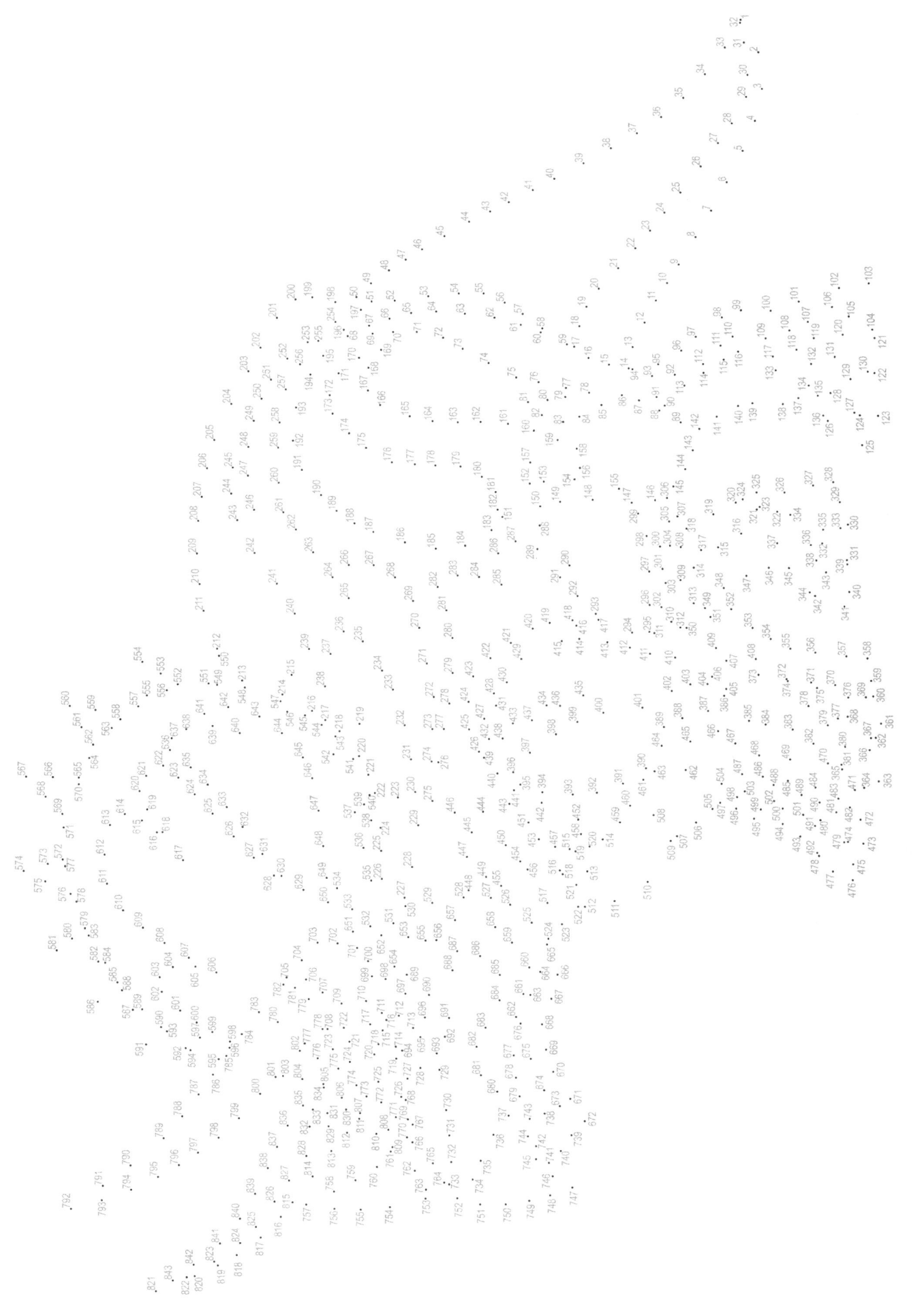

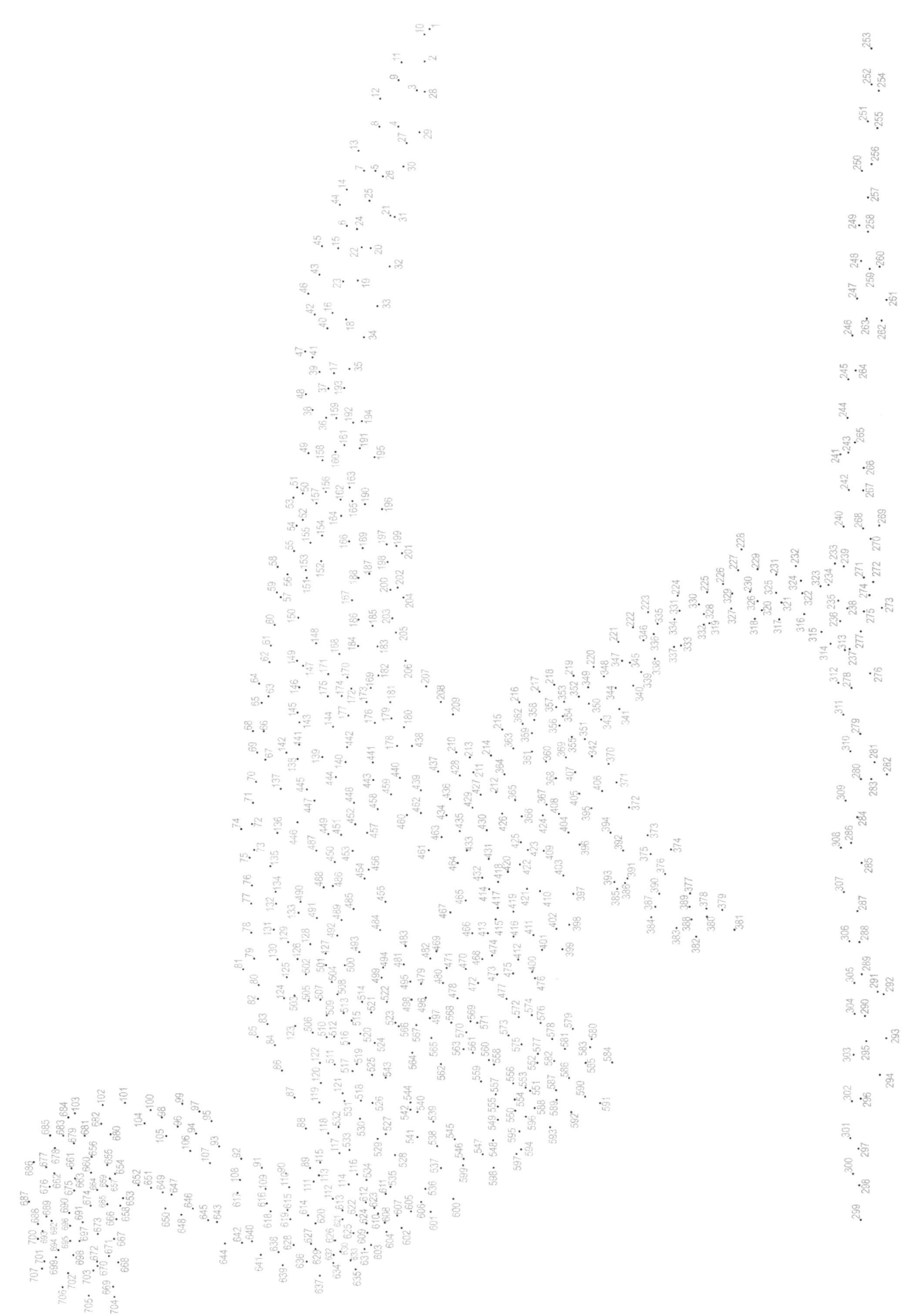

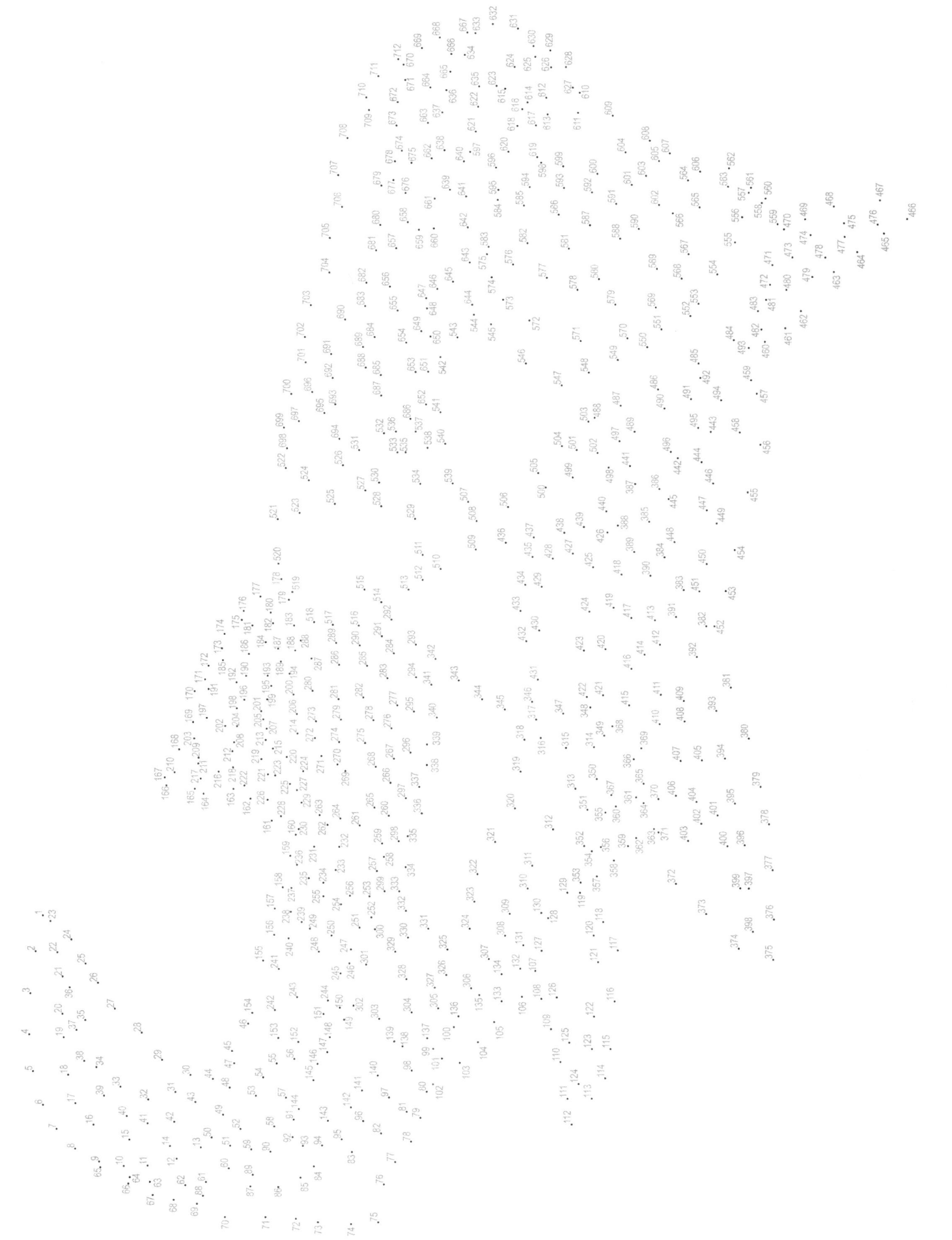

SOLUTIONS

Page 3: Tyrannosaurus

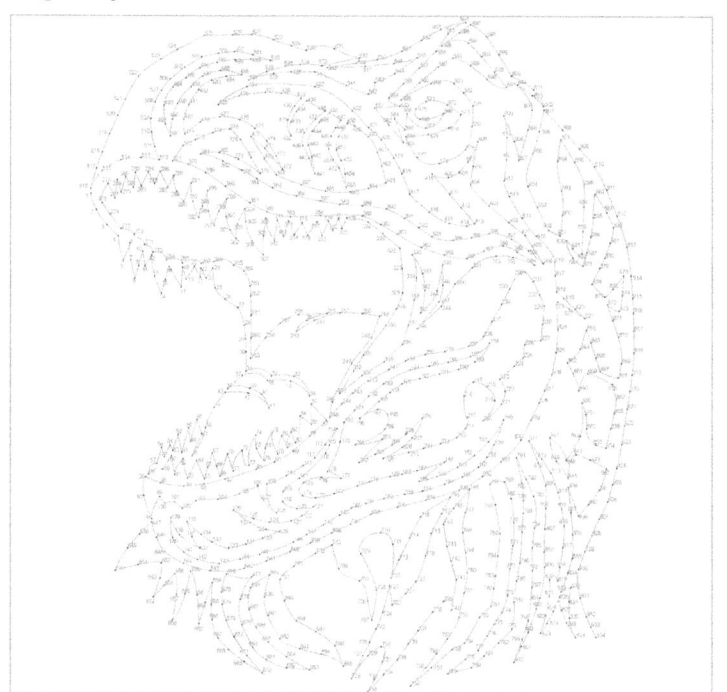

Page 5: Ankylosaurus

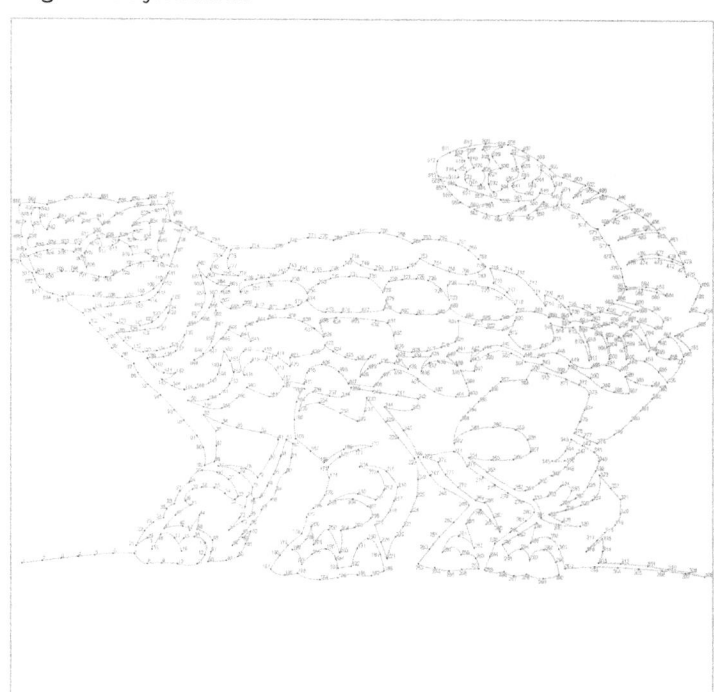

Page 7: Brachiosaurus

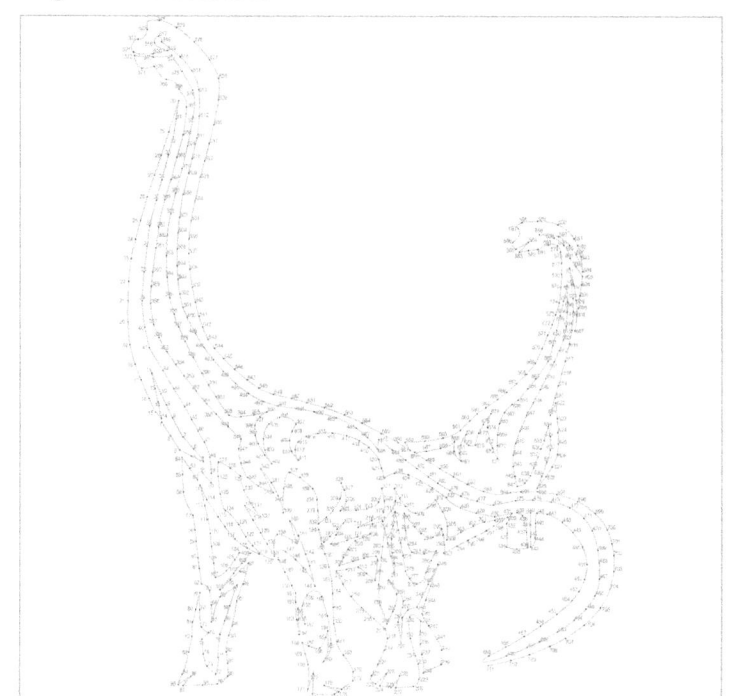

Page 9: Indominus Rex

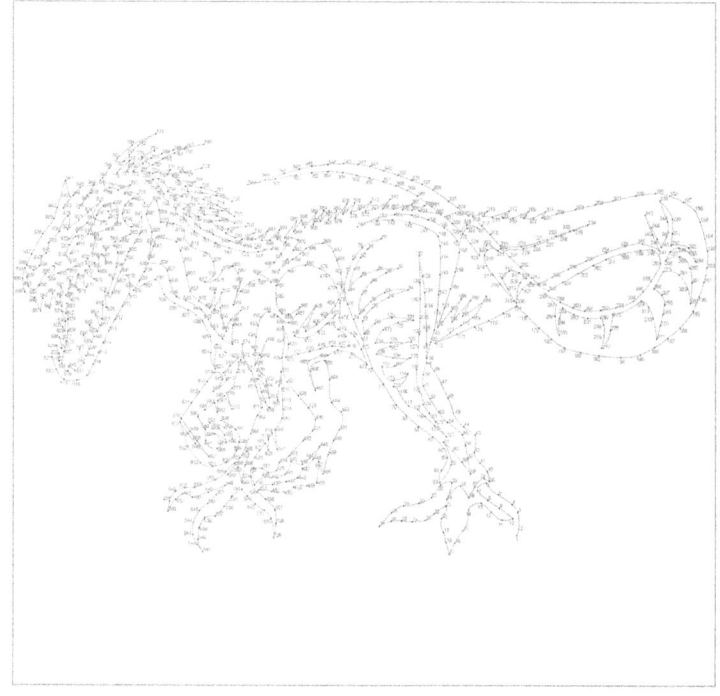

SOLUTIONS

Page 11: Dilophoceros

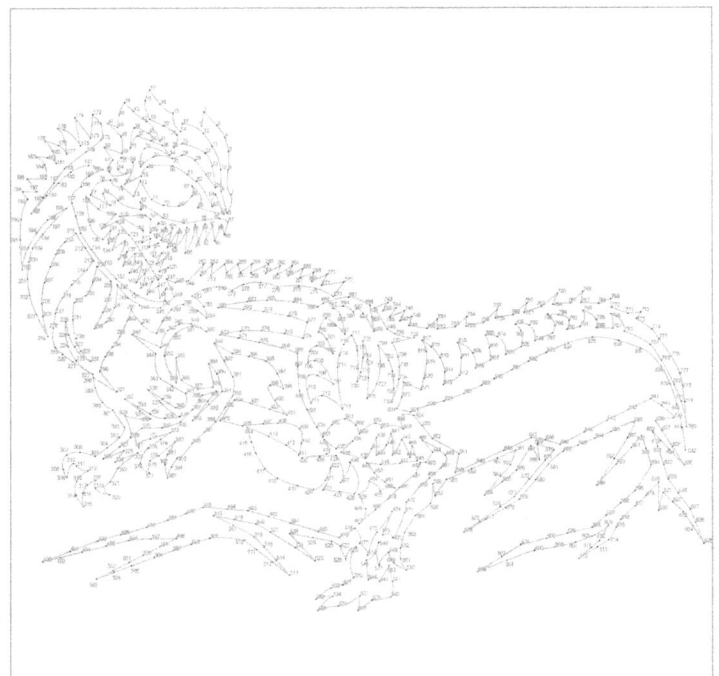

Page 13: Spinosaurus

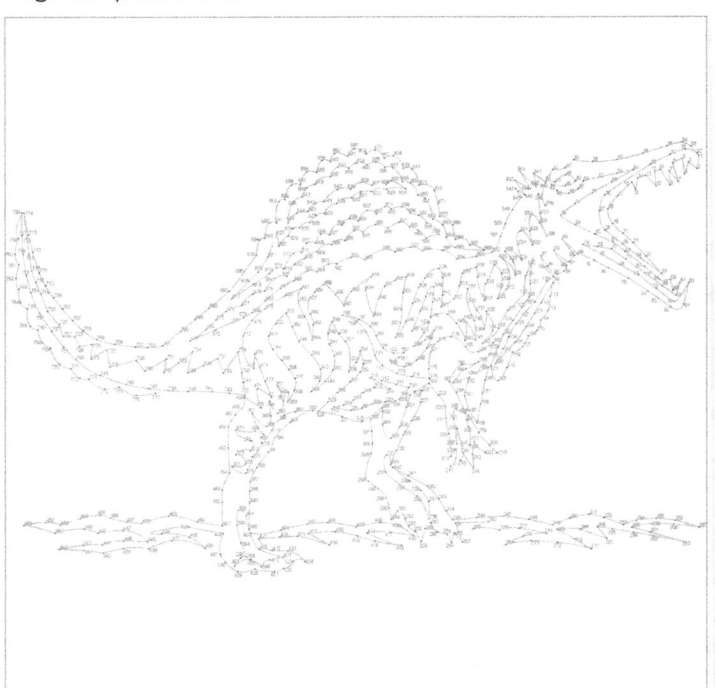

Page 15: Velociraptor

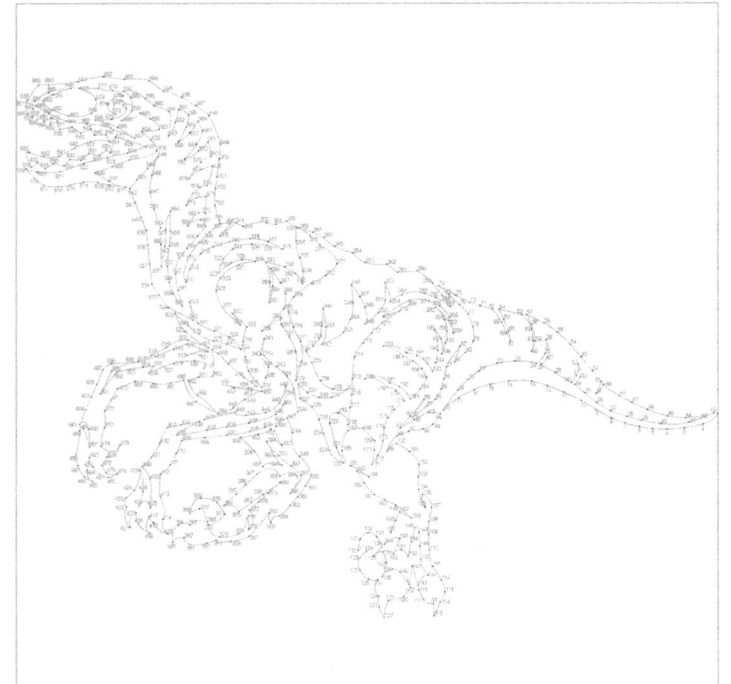

Page 17: Allosaurus

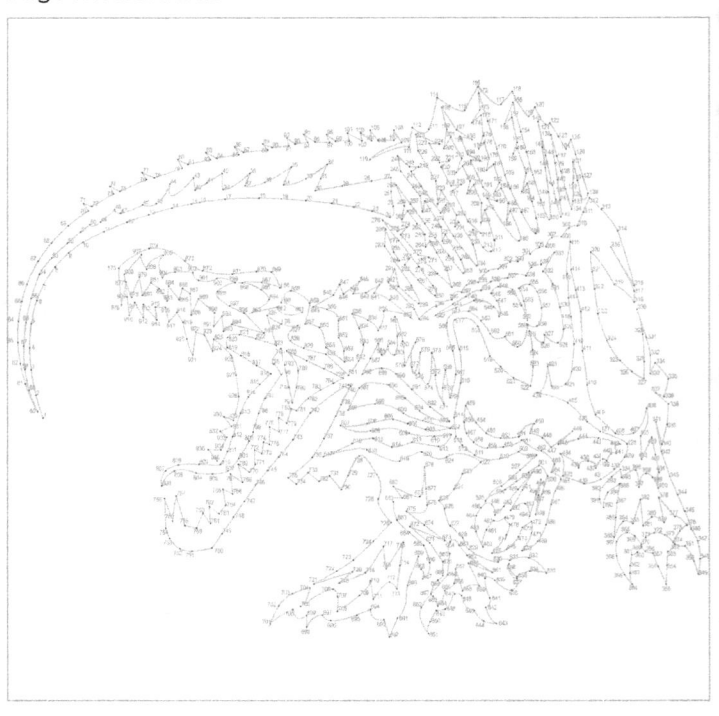

SOLUTIONS

Page 19: Stegosaurus

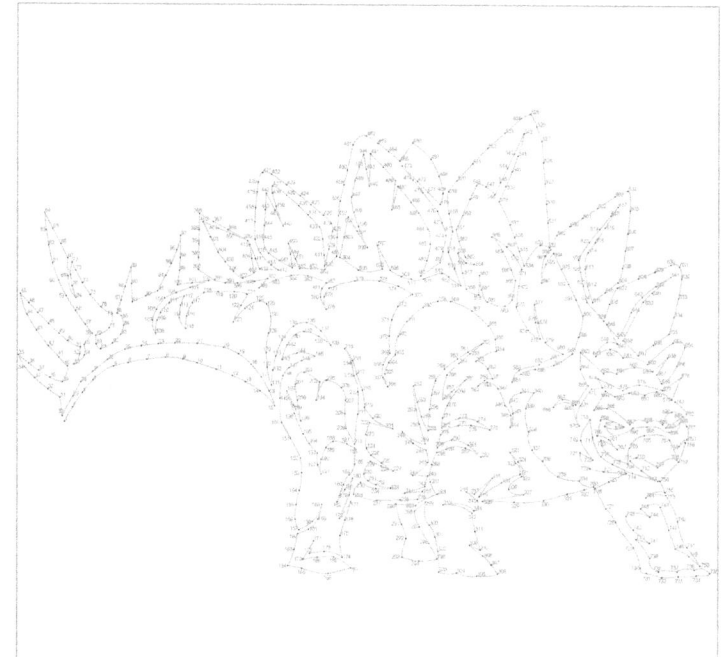

Page 21: Triceratops

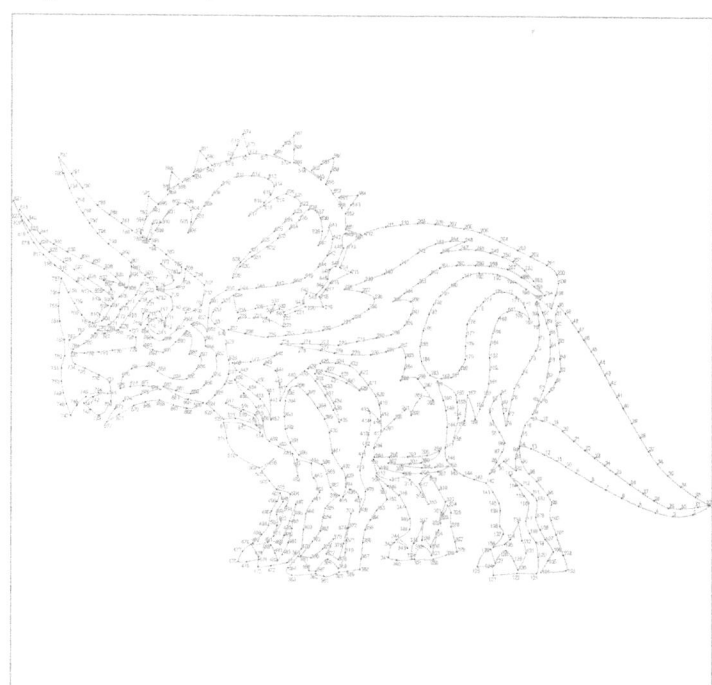

Page 23: Parasaurolophus

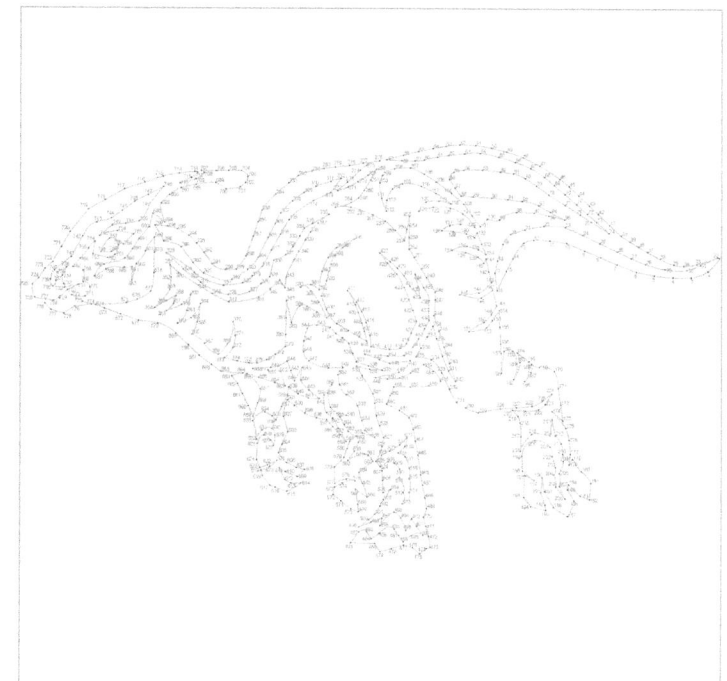

Page 25: Gigantoraptor

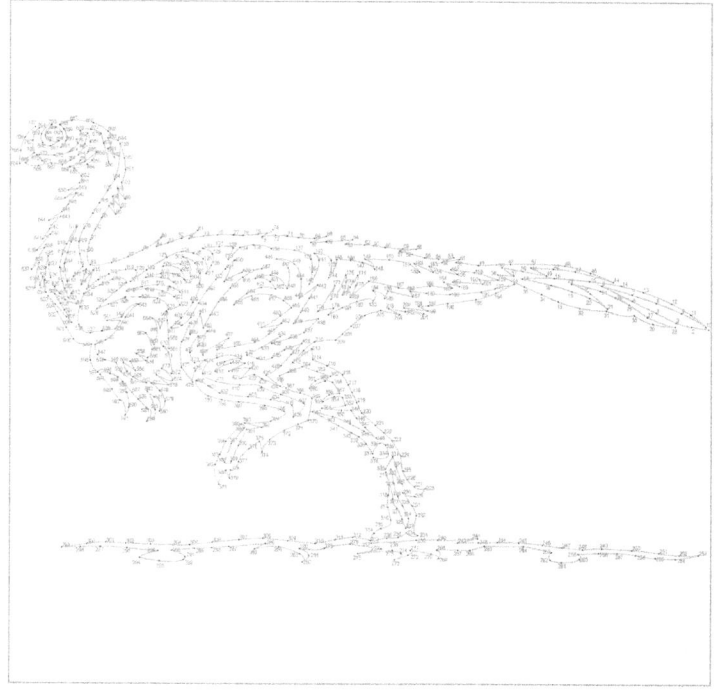

SOLUTIONS

Page 27: Broncosaurus Rex

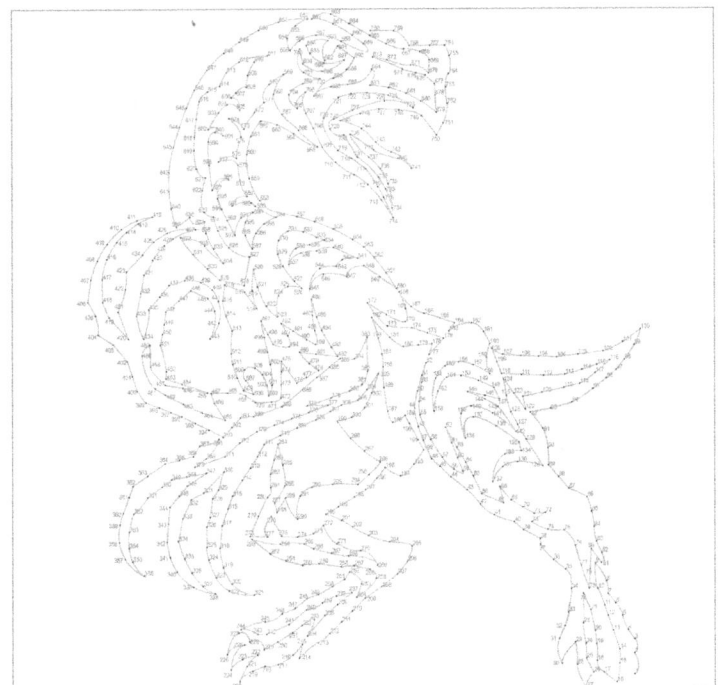

Page 29: Protoceratops

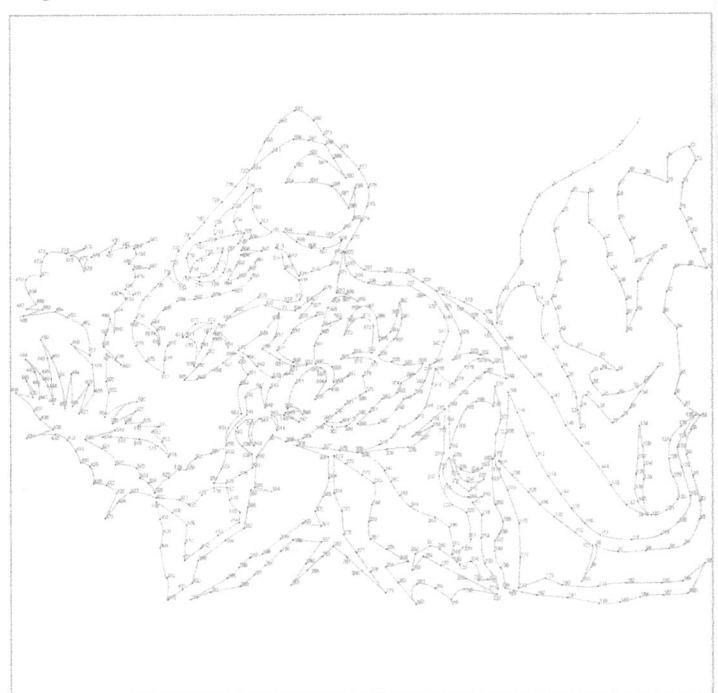

Page 31: Ceratopsians

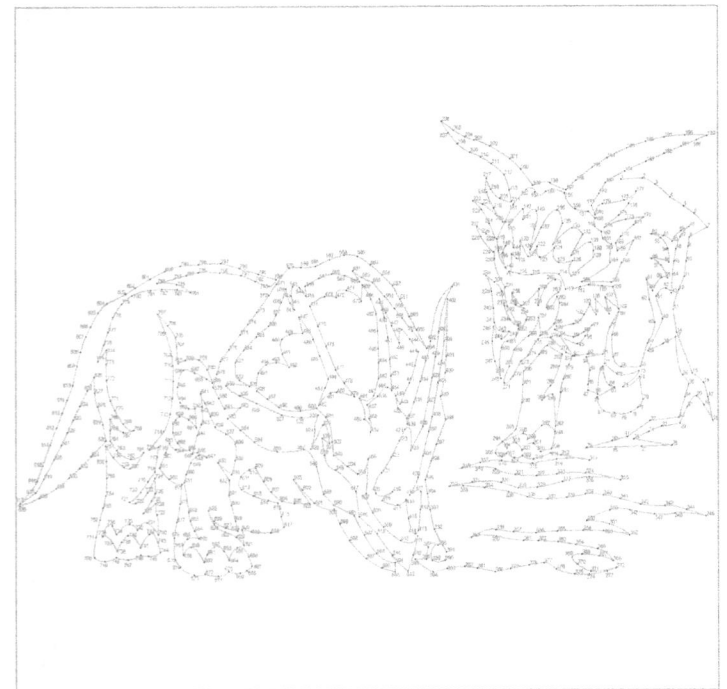

Page 33: Dunkleosteus

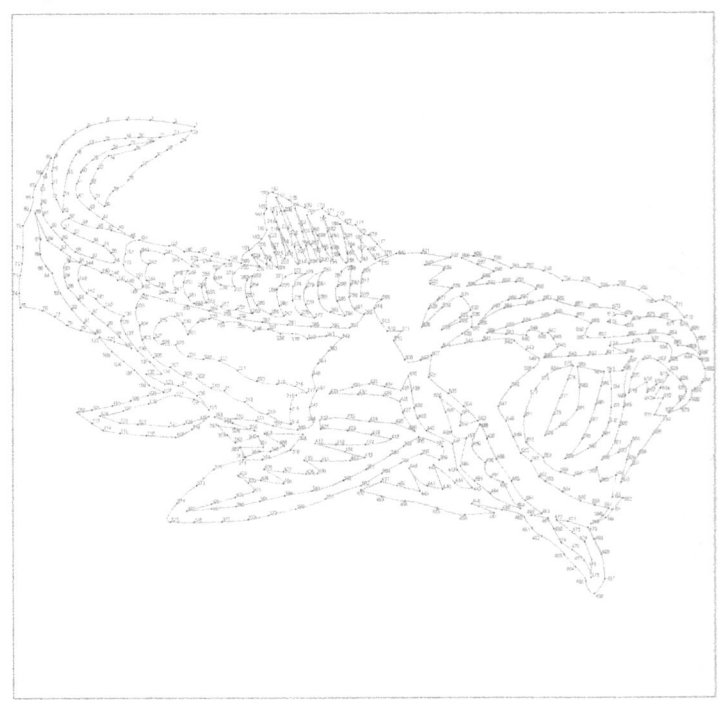

SOLUTIONS

Page 35: Dunkleosteus

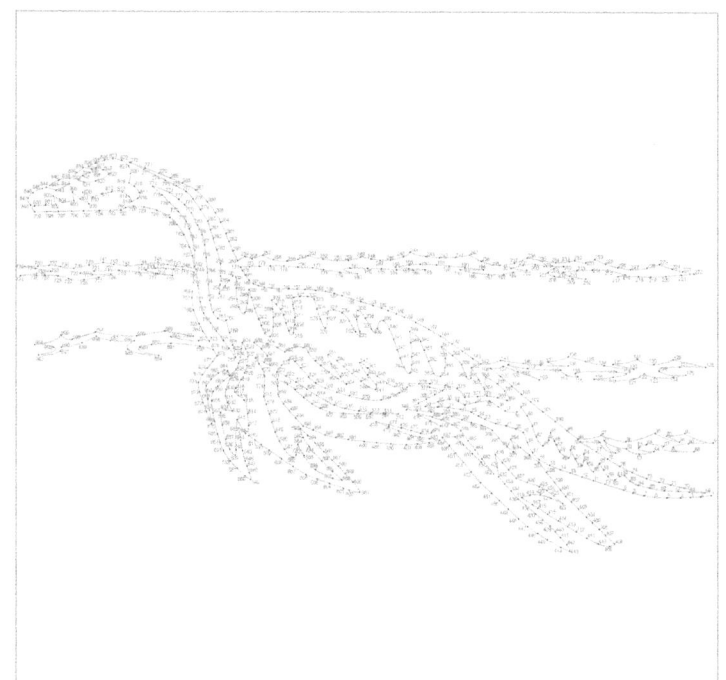

Page 37: Quetzalcoatlus

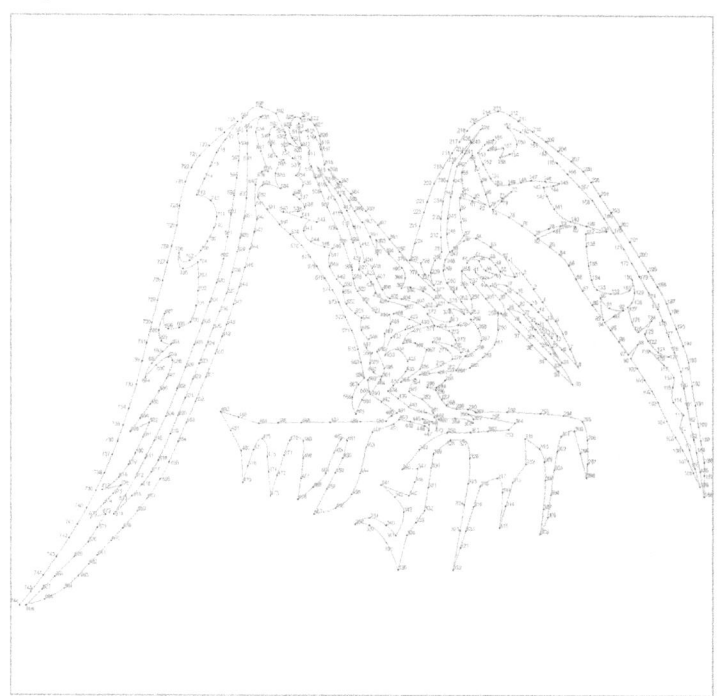

Page 39: Pterodactyl

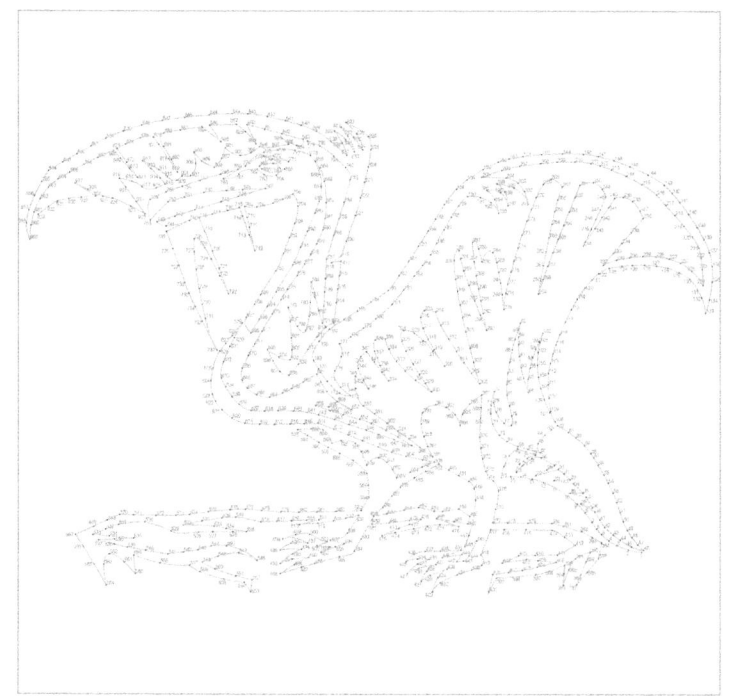

Page 41: Quetzalcoatlus

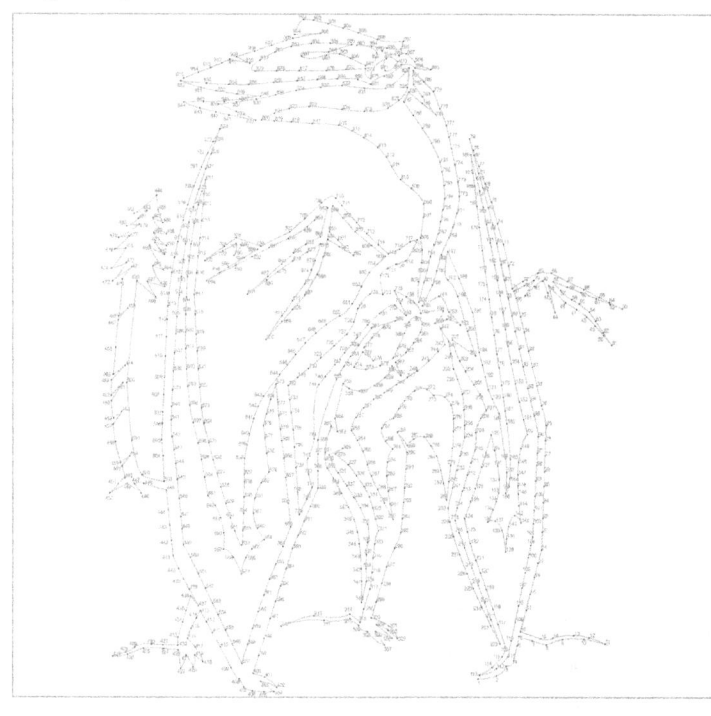

www.ingramcontent.com/pod-product-compliance
Lightning Source LLC
Chambersburg PA
CBHW080911220526
45466CB00011BA/3551